Declutter

A Beginner's 10 Step Guide on How to Simplify Life by Decluttering

I0200876

Other Books by R and R

www.randrdigitallifestyle.com

Table of Contents

Introduction

Have you ever thought how simple your life would be if you didn't have so many things in it? The fact is that less is more, and people are beginning to realize it. The consumerism dream has resulted in more people becoming stressed or being treated for stress-related illnesses and general discontent in most homes. The fact is that we trusted the consumerism dream and bought into it, but the dream is very far from reality. In this 10 step guide, we will show you how to tackle your life and get rid of those things that are not adding value to it.

In our current life, we seldom watch television now, but when we do, we are always amazed at the number of advertisements trying to sell us some new must-have product. You see all kinds of products being introduced onto the market with names you have never heard before, claiming to be better than their predecessors, but when you see advertisements for what they are, you can rise above them and decide for yourself what takes priority in your life. That's the wonderful thing about choice. Over the past 50 years, we have been through enormous changes. If you look at our parents' parents, they made do because they didn't have the choice, but they also didn't suffer from the kind of stresses that people do today. They were not accountable 24 hours a day by cell phone or Facebook, and they didn't have to live up to the standards strewn across all of the front pages of magazines. They didn't care if someone was bigger than average or if someone else was smaller. What they cared about was caring for their family.

At some point, the dynamic changed and home ownership became the catchword of the 80's and 90's, and we began to fill our lives with all the possessions that offered us the chance to be a little bit better off than the people next door. During the 2000's or after the turn of the century, it got worse. People had access to other people over the Internet. There was so much being offered to them. Dial a loan, or get a payday loan! It didn't matter where you got the money from. What mattered was that you had the latest iPhone or that you had the best of what was available. The problem with this equation is that we somehow forgot about all of the crucial things in life. It wasn't about having a happier life. It was all about gratification and instant gratification at that. Be honest. How long did that phone give you entertainment, was it worth the money you paid for it? Looking back at our childhood and the things that made us happy, we wouldn't mind betting that kids in the old days got far more value from a set of pick up sticks than you did from that new expensive investment.

It doesn't end there. There are other areas of your life to declutter. Why? Well, the people you know as friends are not all positive contributors to your life. Do you get used by people? Do you get trampled on by those who think they are superior to you? Well, clearing out the friendship zone is equally important.

In this book, we will deal with all of the things you need to declutter in ten steps. The order in which this is suggested is purposeful. The reason for that is because if you declutter your mind first, the rest gets easier because your brain is ready to say goodbye to anything that has no value in your life.

The minimalist movement in this day and age is winning. People are living in tiny homes. Others are merely living in homes that offer them everything they ever wanted in life, but they have recognized that it isn't the material things that provide you happiness. Home should be a place where you have peace of mind, where you have space to breathe and where you can enjoy your life to the extent of sharing that love with all of those people who are important to you. Instead of being on the gravy train to misery, step into the world of minimalism, and you will soon understand it. It simplifies your life. It simplifies all of the things you have to retain in your head, and it simplifies all of your priorities.

At the end of it all, you have one life to live. Do you want to spend it in debt? Do you want to spend it with people who don't deserve you? How about spending it trying to become better than the people you are jealous of? It's crazy to think that things can bring you any happiness, so take the leap. Take the ten steps and follow us into a better world where you matter, and all of the people within your life add value to it.

Chapter One

Step One – Decluttering the Mind

"The best way to capture moments is to pay attention. This is how we cultivate mindfulness" – Jon Kabat Zinn

Like everyone, we would bet that your mind is ticking away most of the day. It goes over all of the things that have happened to you or all of the worries about things that may occur as a consequence of encounters that you have in life. The first step in this decluttering process has to be the mind. If your mind is filled with stresses and thoughts about everything around you, then how can you enjoy being you? The fact is that you don't need to go through life with all of this clutter in your mind. Think of the clutter as cardboard boxes. Each thought that you have comes from one of these boxes and each time you open up a new thought, you open one of the cardboard boxes, so that at the end of the day you have a mind filled with thousands of open boxes, and therefore the mind isn't free to think what it wants to think. It merely accepts these thoughts as being normal. Perhaps they are normal for you, but you don't have to live with this constant round of negative thought pattern.

You think between 2-3500 thoughts in one hour. That's one heck of a lot of thoughts and feelings running through your brain, and many of these will lean toward negativity. You think the worst of a situation and the mind tends to veer on the side of negativity more than it does on positivity. With all of these thoughts escaping out of their little boxes, there's little wonder that you have time to think about the things that you love doing, or that you want to do to make your world a better place to be. Let's start over and start to clear up what's going on in the mind.

Step One - Clearing the mind

For this exercise, which forms **step 1,** we want you to sit in a quiet place that's at a pleasant temperature and close your eyes for a moment. Breathe in and, as you do so, count to eight and then breathe out and count to ten. The reason you are doing this breathing exercise is to level out the way that you look at life. Your body is excited at times because you have too much oxygen in your lungs or running through your bloodstream and deep breathing of this nature helps to even that out. Keep breathing in this way, and try not to think about anything. It can be impossible at first, so don't get frustrated with yourself for thinking of things. See them as little balloons that are being released into the sky and let go of them without judging them. You can go back to thinking about them when the time is right, but during your session is not the right time.

Without moving from your sitting position, open your eyes, and use all of your senses to grasp this moment. What smells are there? What tastes are there? What can you see that lights up your heart? What about touching something? What does it feel like? Your senses forget all about life when your thoughts are taking over, so sometimes you need to slow down, breathe, and let your senses take over for a while. We would suggest that you do this exercise every morning but that before you do it, you decide where you will do it. Give yourself approximately 15 minutes every morning after you wake to have this "empty space" in your mind and soul. Make this a new daily habit. It gives your mind great clarity, and what you are practicing is decluttering your thoughts. Then, when you find yourself in a situation of doubt or confusion during the day, all you have to do is breathe and close your eyes for a moment, and clarity will return.

During this exercise, you are minimizing the impact of any negative thoughts that may have occurred as you wake. You are allowing positivity to flow over you and you are allowing yourself to see and sense the world around you in a very positive way so that your heart beats slower and your blood pressure diminishes. Take a moment to go back to normal breathing before you get up and start your busy day.

If you want more information on the above techniques, see our Kindle book Meditation for beginners - What is Meditation and how it can

Step Two – Keeping a gratitude diary

The reason we want you to do this is so that you can truly focus on and appreciate the world that you live in and start to think in a very positive way. The moment that you wake reach over for your gratitude diary and write down ten things that you genuinely appreciate in your life in that very moment. The positivity of this action will help you reinforce the benefits of the first step because you know that the breathing exercises will help to clear your mind and that the gratitude diary will help you to start the day with minimal negative thoughts.

It's vital that you start to see the positivity in your life because when you do, you will be more able to let go of the false happiness that you used to get from possessions. You will be able to crystallize that they have little value in your life and be able to distinguish the things and people who genuinely do put joy into your life.

Chapter Two

Decluttering Friendships and Acquaintances

"Fake friends are like shadows. They follow you in the sun but leave you in the dark." Anon

It is normal to over clutter life with possessions but also with people. During the process of decluttering your life, you need to work out who adds value to your life and who does not. Those people who leech from you should be the first to go because they take a lot of mental energy from you and end up making you very unhappy. These steps are all about sorting out your life as far as friends and family go as these are people who may have a considerable influence over the kind of life that you live.

Step Three - Getting Rid of Users

Users are people who offer you false friendship, and in the end, the relationship adds no value to your life. You may dread that person calling. You may pretend you are out rather than answer the door to them. You need to make the decision that you are not going to be used by people. Although it's hard to say "no" at first, you will feel a lot better for it when you get rid of people who don't give anything back to the relationship you have with them. Saying "no" can be a challenging process for some, but you have the right to say no, and you have the right not to have people in your life that do not contribute positively.

So how do you decide?

Make three columns. Write a list of the friends that you have currently in your life. The first column should be for friends you love and that you would never want to disappear from your life. These people give and take and have been with you through thick and thin. The next section is for family members that you are not that attached to and who eat up your energy. If you don't like them particularly, you need to cut down the amount of time that you spend with people of this nature, especially if they give very little back. The third column is anyone who continually asks you to do things you don't particularly want to do. These are the users. They don't give anything back to you and don't appreciate or respect you. These have to be the first to go. The next time that these people telephone for something, you choose to tell them that you are too busy. It doesn't take long for fair weather friends to disappear from your life. There's no need for nastiness. Make it clear that you are not available.

Step Four - Work out your priorities with social events

We are all so "busy." When you fill your life with social events, this can take up a lot of your time, energy, and mindfulness. Decide which activities will give something back to you and give you pleasure and start refusing invitations from people to events that you don't genuinely enjoy. If you have work commitments, you have to balance out whether these refusals will affect your career, but in general, much of what we do with our personal time takes our energy from other more important things. If you don't want to be out all of the time, spend more time relaxing by yourself and with your family. Don't feel bad about not wanting to be involved in everything. People try to dominate our lives and often succeed. If you find that this is happening, start to get your priorities right. The people who matter to you and whose company you enjoy will thank you for it because you will be getting more value from your life.

Step Five - Facebook and online friendships

Facebook and online friendships are becoming more and more common, and the more you see the "perfect picture" of their perfect lives, the less satisfied you become with your own life. Try to minimize friendships on Facebook with people who make you miserable about your life. They are not real friends, and they are not adding any value to your life at all. We often see friends, and family members so pulled into Facebook that they leave many real relationships behind and preferred to have online friendships. We questioned why and realized that they did not want to face what they perceived as their inadequacies. They found online friendships were more comfortable to cope with. This is avoidance. When you sort out real friendships as we have done in the previous steps, you begin to find that life isn't as bad as you might think and that if you mix with the right kind of people more, you will find that you are happier and more at peace with yourself.

If you are single and looking for Mr. or Ms. Right, you have to be right yourself first. So learn to be happy with who you are and the people you mix with, and you will find that positive people are attracted to you and you may even find that one person that means more than all the others put together.

Chapter Three

Decluttering your Workspace and Paperwork

"Clarity of vision is the key to achieving your objectives" Tom Steyer

It doesn't matter if you are a stay at home mom who works on the Internet, whether you live and work full time in an RV or whether you go to an office every day. Clarity helps you make the most of the time that you spend working. That means having things in set places and getting rid of anything that clutters that space that has nothing to do with work.

Step Six - Declutter your working space

Decluttering your workspace means taking the time to figure out what you need and what is distracting in the workspace. If a photo of your near and dear ones fills you with enthusiasm, that's okay, but if it's just taking up space that you could use for work, then ditch it. It is your space to work. You need to make sure that you arrange your papers in such a way that you can find everything, and there are masses of storage solutions around that will help you to do this. It is the same for all of your digital documents and photos. In today's world, there are many solutions available that will provide access to your "digital life." from anywhere.

Decluttering your workspace can start with all the things that are in the drawers of your desk or on the worktop that you never use, or that shouldn't be there. For example, do you have an old piece of equipment that you never got around to repairing? What about files that should have been put away? Are they there for a reason? You need to clear the desk entirely and then start again to introduce the things that are important to your work, discarding those things that get in the way.

You have many workspaces in your home, and you need to review them in the same way, this includes the kitchen – which is a distinct workplace and the laundry room, which is also an integral workspace in your home. There are many areas of your home that will need everything cleared out and evaluated to get rid of things that have been getting in the way of productivity. We have provided these home areas their own space in the chapter relating to your home interior. However, it's worth counting them as working spaces because that's mostly what they are. We fill our lives with too much stuff, and that gets in the way of making progress.

Step Seven – Decluttering your paperwork

Once we had decided that we were going to implement massive changes in our lives and live fulltime in approximately 400sq feet of space we were faced with having to deal with all the "paper" in our life. Going paperless these days is pretty easy, which means that you won't have to file away papers every month, such as utility and bank statements. Ask the institutions that you deal with to go paperless, and you will always have access to the statements or information online. You will still have some paper to deal with, and therefore, you will need a filing system to accommodate the documentation that you need to keep. Example of documents that you may need to keep would be car documents and insurance papers, household accounts, bank statements (from the days before you went paperless), personal documents such as birth certificates, marriage certificates, etc. and paperwork that relates to earnings and tax payments. It's worth having a box or envelops to put receipts in that may be relevant to your current tax year. This will avoid having to spend time during tax season looking for the required documents.

The way to get used to minimizing your paperwork is to deal with letters as they come in. Buy some envelopes and stamps so that when a bill comes in, you can pay it and post the payment straight away. Anything to do with events in the family can be marked onto a calendar and then clipped together so that you can find the relevant paperwork when that event happens. After the event or appointment, you can dispose of the paperwork in the recycle bin or throw it away.

Paperwork in the office

Somedays, you have little control over the amount of paperwork that is continuously sent to you when you work for an employer. You can minimize the clutter by having one tray for papers that you need to deal with (incoming). Another should be marked pending or waiting for someone else's input, and the finally your out tray. Daily, go through each bin and make sure that if anything needs to be passed on to someone else for action, you do it. Once something has been completed, take the time to file the paperwork if it is something that must be kept in hard copy. This will minimize the amount of paper you have in your workspace.

Chapter Four

Decluttering your Home

"The best way to find out what we really need is to get rid of what we don't" Marie Kondo

Your home is the most essential space in your life, so you need to be of a mind to declutter it from start to finish in a set period of time, or you will be in danger of messing up areas that you have already decluttered. For example, if you have a week off work, this could be an ideal time to declutter as it helps you to arrange your life in a better way. Otherwise, you could use weekends but make it a house rule that nothing else gets put in the areas that you have already decluttered. We fill our homes with unnecessary things. How many cell phones do you have in a drawer doing nothing? How many clothes do you have that you don't wear? What about household products that disappointed you? And personal bits and pieces you hold onto because they are sentimental? How many mothers hold onto things that the kids bought or made for them?

Decluttering is an excellent time to evaluate everything, and therefore as your kids will see that you are making a total change to your home, it's unlikely they will notice that you haven't kept that horrible ornament any longer. Remember, it's not about the past. It's about freeing yourself from the baggage of the past and moving forward with only the things in your life that add positivity and joy.

Step Eight – Decluttering your possessions

"Clear your stuff – Clear your mind" – Eric M. Riddle

When you look around your home, you will find that you have a lot of things. We all do. That's the problem with today's society. In every nook and cranny, we keep stuff. Do you remember going to university and starting with a clean dorm, but as time passed and people added more and more to the dorm, it became a place of great chaos which was not conducive to studying? You live your life within the walls of your home and if there is anything in your home that forces you to do extra cleaning or that gets in the way when you have visitors, or indeed that stops you relaxing, it needs to go. We have split this step into different rooms, but before you start, you will need a good supply of plastic storage bags and labels so that you can mark the bags with the following:

- Rubbish

- Give away

- Sell

These are the three ways you have to get rid of things. For example, extra blankets or clothing may be handy for the local homeless shelter as well as food that you know you will never eat. You can sell items marked "sell" via eBay, Amazon, or other platforms, or you could arrange to have a garage sale when you have finished doing the decluttering.

Bedrooms

Actively look at the room. Are there pictures that you don't like? Is there furniture that has no specific purpose? Are there bedclothes that you don't use? Is the furniture too large for the size of the room? What about the window dressings? Are they cumbersome? The idea is to let as much natural light as possible into the rooms to make them appear to be bigger. A large bed could be swapped out for a three-quarter bed in a guestroom since you will only use this room occasionally and there are many stores, which take second-hand furniture and pay you a reasonable amount for it.

Empty the closet and drawers onto the bed. You may want to use a plastic cover over the blankets to stop any dirt getting onto your bedclothes. You need to empty all the hiding spaces so that you can choose to keep those items, which add value in your life. If something makes you look unattractive, or makes you feel miserable, why keep it? The idea of the declutter is to have only things that add value to your life and if you have clothing that no longer fits you all it is doing is reminding you of your failure, get rid of it! If you haven't worn it for the past six months (not merely because of seasonal changes) get rid of it. Get rid of underwear that you don't wear and shoes that no longer feel comfortable because all of these things are filling your closet and drawers with junk, meaning that you have less space to keep things that matter to you.

As you place things back in the drawers and closet, ask yourself whether the item adds to your life. If it doesn't get rid of it, you will be making some money from your garage sale so you can always buy small items that fill gaps or make items into mix and match outfits that you can wear. For the time being, the important thing is to get involved with your possessions and decide upon those that add nothing to your life. If you have rugs in the bedroom and you don't like them, get rid of those too. When you finish a room, it should only have items that give you joy, brings value to your everyday life, and that does not make more work for you on a daily basis.

Children's rooms

If you have children living with you, then you should involve them in the declutter process. Some people say not to include children in the decluttering process, but we believe that they are wrong. Involve them. Children know what they don't wear. They know what they don't play with, and if you simply throw things away, you can cause much resentment. You also have a fantastic opportunity to gather up the things that you believe will be useful for kids that have nothing. There is much that children will learn as they participate in this process as they will come to understand how fortunate they are compared to kids that might not have similar items. The items that the child determines is no longer be required can be cleaned up and donated to a local children's home. Just because you like something, don't insist that your child does. If this decluttering is going to work, it has to involve them so that you all live in harmony after the process is finished.

Bathrooms

You would be surprised how much junk you store in a small room like the bathroom. The problem is that we all buy into the dream that this product will make us look younger or make our hair shinier, and sometimes products don't live up to your expectations. Ditch them or place them into a bag for giving away as these are items that people in a homeless shelter may need. Don't hold onto old medicines because they do eventually go out of date and may be a danger to the unwary anyway. Dispose of them. Drop them off at the local pharmacy, and they will destroy them safely.

Clean out the bathroom and leave products that are fun to use so that everyone participates with the clean-up. Minimize the towels to those that are needed. Clean off the sides of the bathtub and the base of the shower. Introduce something like a squeegee blade, so that cleaning the shower becomes easier for family members. Everyone should participate in keeping the space decluttered and clean.

You can introduce a couple of plants into this area as they thrive in the humidity of a bathroom environment.

Step Nine – Decluttering the kitchen

The kitchen is one job that needs to be a step all on its own because it's a fairly lengthy process. You will need to empty all cupboards and drawers and look for foods that you bought that you will not use. When you moved into the home, the chances are that you thought the kitchen was reasonably large. As you continue to live in the house, the kitchen gets a build-up of excess stuff and now is the time to get rid of it all the un-used and un-needed items. Clean all the cupboards as you go and then look at worktops. These should not be filled up with stuff. It's impractical, and it means that when you need extra room, you have to move things around. We have all bought gadgets that we never use. We all do. Get rid of them and use all the extra space to create a visually larger kitchen. If your cupboards are dark, you may want to make a small investment and paint them all in a fresh coat of paint. If you choose to do this, you will have to remove all of the doors and the drawer fronts and move them to the garage for the painting work to be done. Make sure you have protection on the floor and that you have cleaned all the grease before you paint them. A fresh new color will enhance the look of your kitchen.

Clean out all of the cupboards until there is nothing left in them and make sure that they are clean and dry before deciding what goes where. The freezer and fridge will shock you. The average household wastes so much of what they buy and as you empty the refrigerator and freezer, discard the food that has gone beyond its best by date. You will also find that many items in the freezer are outside of their safe best by dates, so be sure to get rid of them. The idea is always to put newer things at the back and the older items at the front so that you always have food that is in date at all times.

Be careful to label things so that you have expiry dates that you can see. Minimalism means getting rid of excess, but sometimes you can alleviate the guilt of throwing things away by donating them to the needy. They are always in need of food so you won't be wasting it. You will merely be getting rid of things you know you and your family will never eat.

The family room and dining area

In these areas, get rid of the things that you know you won't use anymore. Make sure that the family understands this is not a dumping ground. You need artwork that you love, and the rooms should be welcoming and fresh. Get rid of furniture you no longer use and try to minimize mixtures of colors and patterns. Where are your eyes first drawn when you enter the room? Visitors will tend to notice the same area of the room, and therefore, this is the focal point of each room. If you want to make the most of the rooms, make that space count by having one exceptional item instead of a whole host of photographs or trinkets. If you cannot part with photos or drawings by the kids, then digitize them. Gather all manner of memorabilia and store what you want to pass onto the children up in the loft out of the way. When your home is decluttered, you will learn how to dress it to your liking. All of this decluttering is giving you a second chance at beginning again, and you will be grateful that you changed your mode of life and that you realized that possessions were making your life more miserable. Your home should be somewhere where you can relax, and you may want to change a few colors and get rid of heavy curtains in favor of lighter linen window dressings. A pop of color is always welcome, but when you have too much, it confuses the eye.

The entryway and hallways

Remember that your entryway welcomes people into your home. It shouldn't be cluttered with coats and shoes and things that people put down when they were entering the house. It's a good idea to have a mudroom if you have room for one and to keep the essentials in the hallway. Carefully placed furniture and pictures can make the entryway and hallways look more substantial and more welcoming. The entryway should always be bright and welcoming. If you have a coat stand, make sure it is not cluttered with extra stuff that has simply been dumped.

If you do have a porch, one single plant can make the house look beautiful. Make sure that you don't overdo it. Having loads of pots means more work for you, so keep it easy to clean and welcoming.

The laundry room

The laundry room is an area, which is usually filled up with ironing you will never do and spilled wash powder as well as all of the things that you retrieve from pockets before you wash the clothing. It is an area that needs to be kept clean. If you haven't ironed it in six months, get rid of it because the chances of needing that item are minimal. Wipe off the tops of the washer and try to have a place where dirty laundry can be kept temporarily. It's handy to have a washer and dryer, but if you can go back to simplicity and hang washing outside, do so. It will make your washing smell nicer, and it will cost you less in electricity.

The mudroom

Get rid of the kid's coats that no longer fit them and the old things that have found a home there. If you create colorful pegs for the kids to place their coats and a place for their boots or shoes, kids will usually respond very well to putting things away. In this room, you can also have polish for shoes and brushes, so that once a week, you can all get together and clean up the shoes that have been left there. Once they are dry and clean, they can be transferred to your closets, so that they no longer have to fill up the mudroom. The mudroom should only be a temporary home for wet items and helps to keep the house clean. Storing slippers for everyone in this space will also help to get everyone into the habit of wearing them indoors so that your floors stay nice and clean.

Chapter Five

Preparing for your New Life

"Enjoy the peace of nature and declutter your inner world" – Amit Ray

There is a lot that you can do to minimize stress in your life. Simplify the way that you pay bills, for example, and switch to monthly payments directly from the bank. Switch over from expensive Internet packages and packages that offer you thousands of TV channels because spending more time away from the TV and with the family will enrich your life. These type of changes will also save you a lot of money. There are a lot of items that have value, and these can be sold to help you to make a difference in the way you present your home. The only thing to be aware of is that if you buy something, it should replace something that you already have so that you are not allowing yourself to build up your possessions to the previous state.

Letting the outside in

Nature is a wonderful healer. In Japanese homes, it's not uncommon to see beautiful floral arrangements within the home. These are simple and not elaborate. They make the house look unique and can be incorporated into your home so that you feel that you are relaxed when you are in the space that you call home. There's another way that people can incorporate nature into their lives, which is very useful. If you have French patio doors to the yard, how about extending your living space out into the yard and adding beautiful plants that make the outside seem like an extension of the inside.

Simple seating in this area will make your home seem larger, and this space is something that can be enjoyed by all of the family. A simple vase with a flower in it in areas like the kitchen can make the place smell fresh, and it doesn't cost you anything if you grow flowers in your garden.

Teaching the kids about decluttering

If your home is made up of things that you love, you tend to take better care of them. An efficient way to keeping the rooms neat is always to leave a room tidier than it was when you entered it. This is an excellent practice to instill in your kids. When you see an eight-year-old child straightening a picture because it's the only thing wrong in the room, you cut down on the amount of housework that you have to do, which will free up time to spend with your family. That's a perfect way to look at decluttering. You have less, but you notice it more. Get the kids to help in the design of their bedrooms, and you will learn more about your kids and what they treasure.

Step Ten: The New Things Rule

If you have been through all of the steps so far, step ten is an essential one for everyone who lives in your home. For every new item that you buy, you need to remove something that is already in the house so that the kids get to understand that it's a case of choosing to make room for the new things that mean more to them. You can usually get kids onboard by having a garage sale of their older items, which gives them a little bit of savings toward new things. We all like to buy things and going to the supermarket puts you in reach of temptation. Make it a habit to take take a list with you so that you don't buy things that you do not need. Supermarkets are very talented at tempting customers, and you will end up with cupboards overflowing with stuff if you don't abide by the rules. As far as food goes, try to introduce fresh foods, but never buy too many because they will spoil more quickly and it becomes a false economy.

The idea now is to make sure that people put things away in your home. Your home will be a lot less busy, and you will find that you have more time on your hands to do the things that you want to do, instead of feeling overwhelmed by the mess you have created as a family. Minimizing allows you to explore what you do love and to do more of those things together. We learned that we enjoyed photography as we went through each room of our house and previously had no time to improve what we were producing. Now we can sell many images to online websites which were willing to pay for them!

You need to watch less television. This is a huge influencer when it comes to buying into the 21st century. If your phone works, you don't need a new one, and you certainly don't need to be reminded that yours is out of date all the time. Use the time that you have to enjoy family time instead of mindlessly being told that you need to buy into the dream.

As a tip to help you to get space back into your life, light colors appear more spacious, and if you make the transitions between rooms easy on the eye, this also helps you to make the home a more relaxing place to be. You will find that your tastes change over time and if this happens, replace the artwork with what makes you relaxed and happy instead of merely adding to it. Let us show you an example. You have a collection of vases that you like. Place them onto a shelf and look from a distance. They may not make much impact. Now try this. Choose your favorite and place it where it can be appreciated, and you will notice it more. The reason for this is that clutter obscures the view and you begin to take it all for granted and not see what's important to you anymore.

Less is always more, and as you get to live in your space without all of the clutter, you will find that your stress levels go down and that you can relax more which is what your home is supposed to do for you. You may find that people around you start to envy the calm of your home and want to copy you. It is also interesting that many people who declutter their homes turn a new leaf and start taking more time with their meals together and start to communicate instead of avoiding each other at meal times.

Involve the kids in your life and be involved in theirs in this new decluttered home and you will find that not only is your life calmer, but you also free up time to enjoy family things together. For example, the calendar upon which you mark up and coming events could be brought out at breakfast time each day, so that you all know what's going on and don't have to worry about forgotten appointments, visits to school or visits to the dentist. Be on the same page as your kids, and you really will enjoy life more. Minimalism doesn't mean going without. It means having more of so many things that you may not have appreciated at the beginning of the exercise. Now that you do know what it's all about, no doubt you will enjoy life more and find that your work life and home life are both equally enjoyable and rewarding. All of the money that you save during this process can help you to have vacations to places you always wanted to go because you are not prepared anymore to spend money on things that don't mean very much, beyond the half hour or so of novelty that new items give you.

Since decluttering our lives, we have more time to do things, less stress and worry about maintenance and repairs and we get to enjoy more time together There is so much more to life than going home to a cluttered home and having to do chores. Once your home is organized, you have so much more time in your life to do things that add to your life instead of things that add to your worries.

Conclusion

So, you have read this far, but we doubt that you have made the move toward decluttering your life yet. We would ask you to go back over the contents of this book and work out which were is the best place for you to start. You will never really look back with regret when you decide to declutter. Much of the possessions that you have hold you back from enjoying your life. You end up spending hours vacuuming around these items and having to dust them! With a feather duster, we can keep our home clean without the effort of putting a whole morning aside to do that work.

We have also made it simpler for the kids to put things away, confining their toys to a large box, and creating comfortable hanging spaces for their clothing. You can do that as well and find yourself spending much less time nagging your kids to keep their rooms tidy. At the end of all of this sorting, you need to donate, throw away, or sell the items that you have decided no longer form a part of your life. We feel that the best way of doing this is to sell them at a garage sale and then donate anything that's left. Be careful, however, that you are not tempted to bring things back into the home once you have decided to say goodbye to them. If you do have doubts about specific items, place them into a box marked doubts, and put this into the garage or wherever you have to store them. If you haven't touched them within a set amount of time, get rid of them. They are not adding to your life.

The reason that we are so passionate about teaching people to declutter is that it has made an enormous difference in our lives. We know that our life is more vibrant because of it. We went to extremes, but it has given us a lifestyle to is genuinely free from everyday stress that we would recommend it to everyone. Home baked cookies are far more enjoyable than packaged ones, and you get a chance to do these things with your family and friends so that the purpose of home baking takes on a whole new meaning.

A very invigorating process!

When your home offers you more space, you feel less hemmed in by it all. When we made the decision to sell our house and business and to move into an RV, we worried about what to do with many of our possessions. Once we started the process and genuinely committed to downsizing to a much smaller space, we found that we really needed very few of the items that were in our home, garage, or basement. When you get to this stage, you can relax and enjoy life more, and now we no longer have to work so hard to finance a costly lifestyle. We now have more time together to enjoy life and to travel more as we no longer have to worry about the house staying empty while we are away. Taking away the possessions and the necessity to keep up with everyone else will change your life forever. You have to decide at the end of the day what you want out of life. Do you want to have all the latest gadgets and no life, or would you rather have a life and a few items that mean a lot to you?

Decluttering allows you to start life over again. We often wondered how people who traveled a lot managed to live out of a suitcase, but we understand now that they made a choice themselves to live that way because they wanted to travel. We, on the other hand, wanted a simpler life, where we weren't always taxed by problems and stress, which can indeed lead to heart attack and early death. With our priorities in order, we get to spend our time now as we see fit and do things like creating e-books. Please do reread the book and be sure to follow the steps because once you do, you will find that life offers you so much more than it is offering you right now. It isn't worth losing your happiness for the sake of things. As we look at our home these days, we know that the inner joy and contentment we feel was through our own choices. You too can choose, and when you do, you will wonder why you didn't do it earlier in your life.

We wish you well with your decluttering and hope that you find all of the happiness that you seek. If you don't, then you need to assess what you want out of life and go for it. Sometimes it takes decluttering to help you to find a new direction that helps to improve your life and the experiences in it. Less will always be more. Believe it. Declutter and find your way through the maze that life presents to each human being in the 21st century. Once you do, you will never look back and wonder why you did it.

If you enjoyed this book or found it useful, please leave a review on Amazon.

We hope that you enjoyed this book – Thanks for reading - Ray & Ruby – A Simpler Life